To

PAMELA KEILY

This play was commissioned by the Committee for Religious Drama in the Northern Province, and was first produced by Pamela Keily with an amateur company, The Wayfarers, at the Leeds Civic Theatre, in October 1961. The plot is based on an actual incident in a car park in Germany, which was reported in *The Times*.

Who is My Neighbour?

and

How Bitter the Bread

by the same author

★

THE TRIAL OF THOMAS CRANMER

THE SHADOW FACTORY: A NATIVITY PLAY

HENRY BLY AND OTHER PLAYS

★

A MATTER OF LIFE AND DEATH

THE GOLDEN BIRD AND OTHER POEMS

★

edited by Anne Ridler

BEST GHOST STORIES

Who is My Neighbour?

and

How Bitter the Bread

by

ANNE RIDLER

FABER AND FABER
24 Russell Square
London

First published in mcmlxiii
by Faber and Faber Limited
24 Russell Square WC1
Printed in Great Britain at
The Bowering Press Plymouth

Contents

Who is My Neighbour?

A Play in Three Acts

CAST

JANET BRACE: a girl of about twenty

PAUL SQUIRE: a trainee manager, in his early twenties

MRS. BRACE: Janet's mother

ROBERT BRACE: Janet's brother, about nineteen

NELLO ROSSI: an Italian waiter

JACK: a young factory worker

ONLOOKER: a clerical worker

DETECTIVE-INSPECTOR JOHNS

The first and third Acts are set in the BRACES' sitting-room, which reflects ROBERT's taste in interior decoration.

The second Act is in the saloon bar of the Merry-Thought, a road-house. There are a few small tables for meals, and a window at the side or back is supposed to open on to a yard for parking.

ACT I

The Living Room of the Braces' House

PAUL *is alone in the room: he is very nervous: fidgets about; settles with magazine; gets up, and is just straightening his tie in the mirror when* JANET *enters.*

JANET: Good evening. I'm so sorry to keep you waiting.
I hope our Danish girl didn't show you into the cellar?

PAUL: Yes, as a matter of fact she did, at first!

JANET: O dear! She always thinks that anyone who calls,
At whatever time of day, has come to read the meter—
She thinks that we measure out our lives by therms—
Men have died, and therms have eaten them . . .
That's what she must think. And I have to confess
That she didn't catch your name.

PAUL: Paul Squire, from Brace Electric. Could I speak to Mrs Brace?

JANET: I'm afraid my mother is out,
But if it is a message from my father, perhaps
You could give it to me? I am Janet Brace.
I don't suppose it is anything very private?

[*As* PAUL *does not answer, she continues.*]

It's a novelty to see someone here from the Works.
You wouldn't believe how little we know
About anything down at the factory.
I believe you are the first one to visit this house
From Brace Electric. But do sit down.
A cigarette?

PAUL: No, thank you, not just now.

JANET: What do you do there?
What's your particular job, I mean.

PAUL: I'm a management trainee. That is to say
I hope—or I *hoped*—to manage a department
Later. At the moment I'm learning the job:
I'm going through the Works—spending a few months
In each department.

JANET: That must be very interesting.
I've often wished that I could go into the business,
But my father wouldn't hear of it.

PAUL: Really?

JANET: Not a job for girls, he said. He may come round,
But at present—nothing doing. So I'm going to train
As a physio-therapist: I shall like that.
Do you enjoy your job? I don't suppose
My father is good at deputing work:
He's always so clear about things himself,
And so very much alive to . . . [*a movement from* PAUL] O, I'm talking too much
As usual. You came with a message from my father,
And you haven't been able to get a word in edgewise. . . .

PAUL: Your father . . . Your father will not be home to dinner.

JANET: He sent you to tell us? How very extraordinary.

PAUL: No, *he* didn't send me. He has been—called away.

JANET: Called away?

PAUL: An accident.

JANET: What sort of accident?
O, don't say he has run someone over?

PAUL: No, it wasn't that.

JANET: He's not tender to fools,
And we're always afraid he will drive into someone
To teach them to look where they are going. Then
Something at the factory?

PAUL: Not at the factory.
I can't tell you much, because I wasn't there—
Really I wasn't. I had gone away
Before it happened—I mean, I was never there.
I heard about it—didn't I say that?—
When I returned for overtime. They sent me to tell you—
Or rather, it was Mrs Brace I was to tell.
I wish I could speak to her.

JANET: She went out shopping
With my brother, and I don't know when she will be back.
I think you had better have a cigarette, you know:
I see it's something bad. Now, take your time:
You have something bad to tell me. Isn't that it?

PAUL: Yes, I am afraid so.

JANET: My father is hurt?

PAUL: I have to tell you that your father . . . [*he pauses*]

JANET: He is dead?
Please do tell me exactly what has happened.
It is far worse to be fed with crumbs of truth
Than the whole bitter piece. Tell me.

PAUL: He died
At once, without suffering. I am sure of that.
Of course I wasn't there, but from what I know
I am sure of it. It seems that your father
Had gone into a place called the Merry-Thought—
It's not far from the factory—he often went there.
His car had been parked in the yard next the bar;
He went out to get it and . . . well, just imagine
How it might have happened: the pavements are icy,
The fog is like an ether pad today—stings your eyes
And bewilders your brain—he might easily have slipped,
Or a car was backing and knocked him over—

That could have been it—anyhow, he fell,
And a wheel must have gone over him.
O, I am a brute:
They sent me to break the news to you gently,
And I've done it so clumsily—please forgive me.

JANET: Gently? How can the truth be told gently?

PAUL: I don't know. I could not think how to say it—

JANET: He is dead, you say.

PAUL: He must have died without pain.

JANET: Only lies are gentle. If you had said
'Your father is hurt, but will soon recover';
Or 'Your father has gone on a journey'; or else
'Your father took wings and flew up to the sky'—
That would have been gentle; that is what they mean
By 'breaking the news gently'. But the truth is always harsh,
And I almost think that whatever is not painful
Is not the truth. You said he must have died without pain:
How can you possibly know?

PAUL: It must have happened so quickly.

JANET: That's what we think. But I've been told—I have read—
There is room in an instant for eternities of pain.
All the pain of life could be gathered in that moment
While the wheel went over. And while he perished,
Not a throb disturbed us—not a wave reached us;
We walked about, and washed up the dishes, and chattered.
He died quite alone. How can it be
Mr Squire? How can we be so deaf and senseless
As to feel nothing while a man is dying?

PAUL: You mean telepathy?

JANET: Nothing so grand.
Not even love, I think. I mean just—relationship.
If I can feel the merest scratch for myself,
How could I not feel Death strike my father?

PAUL: I was never near enough to anyone
To think that I should feel their pain. But I suppose
You were very close to him?

JANET: He was my father.
Was? no, he still is. I never considered it.
Love for one's father is less difficult, you know,
Than love for one's mother—with a girl, that is.
I was proud of him, certainly: he was so successful
In everything he did; what he could not do well
He never attempted. It seems so unlike him
To blunder into a car in a fog.
I can't make myself believe it has happened.
That's why I'm talking like this, as though
It were somebody else. But I feel . . . I feel
As though I had failed him.

PAUL: But what could you have done?

JANET: O, nothing. Of course you're going to say I wasn't there.
But he was my father: a part of his life
Is in me, and I did not even guess that he had died.
How closely we live in our own stone prisons!

PAUL: It is hard enough to bear without such thoughts.
Surely life would be unendurable
If we were joined to others by such a fine web?

JANET: O—never mind if you can't understand.
I'm still half in a daze. Is there something I must do—
Sign any papers—identify . . . I hope not.

PAUL: No, O no. It has all been done.
But we have to tell your mother.

JANET: And then there will be an inquest.

PAUL: But you won't need to go. Neither of us will.

JANET: You will not, certainly, since you could tell them nothing.

PAUL: No, I could add nothing to what they know.

JANET: Have you really told me all you know? the Merry-Thought . . .
I think I have been there. A sort of road-house
Isn't it? Lots of plush and chromium;
An expense account sort of place?

PAUL: Yes, that's it.
And it has a public bar as well,
Rather less posh.

JANET: He went to get his car . . .
There'll be medical evidence—horrible miracles
Of reconstruction . . .

PAUL: I don't see why there need be:
An accident, in fog . . . do you really think there will?

JANET: Well, it won't affect you, if there is. But his death may?
If he was training you . . .

PAUL: Did he ever mention me?

JANET: He didn't talk much about the office, as I said,
Though he lived for his work, of course. Really, I suppose,
He preferred to have his worlds divided by an ocean—
An ocean of silence. Our continent was tiny
Compared with Brace Electric! Like England to America.
I do remember, though, that he said he intended
To take on an assistant. We wondered a little,
Because of Robert.

PAUL: Who is Robert?

JANET: He's my brother.

PAUL: I never knew that Mr Brace had a son.

JANET: Eighteen months younger than me. And much cleverer,
Only he never works at anything.
He's up at Oxford, reading modern languages.
It wasn't *his* idea—he wanted to travel,
And Dad would have liked him to go in for science:
They compromised on this; and in the long vacations
He gets abroad as a courier.

PAUL: Why did we never hear of him, I wonder?

JANET: I don't think my father wanted Robert in the firm,
For whatever reason.

PAUL: I can guess the reason.
To have a son around would have cramped his style.
And he wouldn't want his son to see . . .

JANET: Well, to see what?
Go on, you must finish what you started to say.

PAUL: Your father was not a very popular employer . . .
But I don't want to speak of that now. . . .

JANET: No, tell me.
I know my father could be ruthless; and then
There were some things he never understood; in some directions
One came to a wall with 'No Through Road'
Written very large. But if you didn't try
To push past those notices, he was always fair to you.
He was a *just* man.

PAUL: Yes, I suppose so.

JANET: You had a grievance against him? Tell me.
I want to know how he seemed to people
Who met him in his work.

PAUL: Well, I will try.
But now that he is dead . . .

JANET: Go on. How did you happen
To start in his factory?

PAUL: He came to my school
To give away the prizes, and afterwards he talked
To us prefects. O, the way he described
The openings in industry, the work of his firm!
He made it sound like conquering Everest.
As you said earlier, it was all so clear—
The career went up and up like a graph.
And so when he offered me a job—why
I thought I'd got a chair in the Board Room already.
O, I was green! It was all so different
From what I had expected.

JANET: But that wasn't *his* fault?

PAUL: No, not exactly. But before I started work
He seemed to be aware of me as a person—
I thought so, at any rate. As soon as I started,
I was just part of the machine. He expected me
To get things right without any help.
If all went well, nothing was said,
Never a word of praise or encouragement.
If things went wrong—I was a moron,
He couldn't think why he had given me the job,
And so on!

JANET: He didn't care for praise himself,
And he never could imagine another person's feelings:
It wasn't in his power.

PAUL: And then the factory.
What were we making? Switches and sockets.
But to hear your father talk, you'd have thought we were forging
A hub for the universe to turn on: we *were*
The hub of the universe. I couldn't feel it:

I couldn't see that a few thousand plugs
Either more or less were of any importance.
I couldn't treat my work as a dedication—
If I'd felt like that, I'd have gone into a monastery.
And I felt so isolated. The men weren't unfriendly,
But I was betwixt and between—not a boss,
Nor exactly one of *them*. I got bored with their grumbles—
They felt it. And then the din! It was frightful.
They said I'd soon get used to it. I couldn't hear my thoughts:
I began to talk aloud to myself outside
Just to make sure that my voice was still working.
I asked Mr Brace if I could try another section
Just for a week or two. He didn't even answer.
I thought I was going mad. And then this evening . . .
But he is dead.
I keep forgetting that: it shows one, doesn't it,
How much he dominated everything?

JANET: Yes.
I expect he was disappointed. You were in the wrong job,
Don't you think so? and he saw it. He never made allowances.
He expected people to use their last electron
Of energy, as he did himself.

PAUL: For the glory
Of Brace!

JANET: You've no right to say that! You have told me—
You just crumpled up when you found that a factory
Isn't a paradise. What could you know
Of his motives, or his worries? I don't suppose you dream
What a strain a modern Director has to take.
Just a beginner, you were, just a run-about. . . .
I'm sorry: I didn't mean to be rude.

I thought I was very detached and objective
About my father—I liked to criticize him,
But I see that it has to be *my* prerogative,
I can't take it from anyone else.
That is very stupid. I do understand,
I see that he did make you suffer. Only—
People with a factory to manage nowadays
Do have frightful anxieties, live
In a constant crisis: you might make allowances
For that?

PAUL: You looked like your father for a moment
When you were angry; but otherwise—no.
You aren't at all like him; this room isn't like him.
I expected to find his house made to his shape,
Like a cast in the sand.

JANET: Perhaps you would see that in his study; this room
Is really Robert's cast: he chose the colour scheme.
He's got his own taste, as you see. And he buys
All kinds of oddments that I should never notice
And brings them home, and they look just right.

PAUL: Is that his photograph?

JANET: No, that was Daddy
As a boy.

PAUL: I should never have thought it.

JANET: No?
I have seen that face, within his, occasionally,
Like a bright shell, deep in a pool.

PAUL: If I had known him at home, with you,
I see I should have known a different person.
And to find it out now—and you—after what happened. . . .
You can't understand what I'm trying to say,
But O, if today had never been!

JANET: Useless to think of it.
[*She notices packet on table.*]
Did you bring this?

PAUL: Some things he had with him
Which I was to return.

JANET: How homeless they look without an owner! This watch
That I used to pull at when I was little
And blew to make it open.
O, these make me feel that he is really gone.
[*She weeps.*]
I didn't, until now.

PAUL: O dear.
I wish I knew what to say to comfort you.
I'm so useless. You make me feel
For the first time, just what a worm I am—
A worm and a coward. I wish I had died
Instead of your father—I do indeed—Janet.
If I had known you before . . . before it happened
I could have had the courage . . .

JANET [*who was hardly listening*]: You are very kind
Mr Squire . . .

PAUL: My name's Paul.

JANET: Paul then. It's so stupid of me,
But looking at those things, I feel he must need them:
I feel that he'll be lost without his pocketbook
His papers and his money—I wonder how he'll manage!
All his arrangements upset—his hold on life
Struck away. I understand now how it was
That people used to bury precious things with the dead.

PAUL: They still do, you know. And the people who die—
They will to be buried in wool, or to carry
Their General Certificates—pass in five subjects—
But he needs nothing any more.

JANET: He needs
The love of God. O, he was not ready to die.

PAUL: At the moment when that photograph was taken, he looks
As though he were ready. Why do men grow up?
O, don't cry, dear Janet.

JANET: Please take no notice.
I hate to be watched crying.

PAUL: I would give anything
To have the right to comfort you now. I would give
Anything to . . . [*he seems about to kiss her, but draws back*]
No, you won't look to me for comfort.

JANET: I might look to you for a dry handkerchief.
Thank you. I'm better now.
You've been very kind. You say that he looks
Fit for heaven, in that photograph? But I wonder, do you think
That the best of ourselves, at any given moment
In *any* part of life, is the truest, and it might be
That this is what survives when we die?

[*Voices in the hall.*]

O dear, they are back. My eyes—what shall I do?

PAUL: After my own bungling, I don't know what to say,
But you told me, it is easier to have the whole truth
At once . . .

JANET: Yes, for me, but not for my mother.
She likes things muffled. We must tell her gradually.
Help me—Paul.

MRS BRACE [*in the hall*]: Open the door, Janet dear, I'm laden.
[*entering*] We've had a good day, though the fog was dreadful.

ROBERT [*entering*]: I thought it was delicious—like minestrone.

JANET [*behind the door*]: This is Paul Squire, from the factory, Mother.
He has something to tell you.

MRS BRACE [*putting down parcels*]: Now I can shake hands! Did you want my husband?
I thought he was down at the Works himself.
This is my son Robert. [*They shake hands.*]

JANET [*her back turned*]: Mother, I have to . . .
Did you have a good day?

ROBERT: She has just told you so.
I can't wait to show you the cloth we chose.
There—what do you think of that? Isn't it divine?
With either of these ties—those were an extravagance.

MRS BRACE: They certainly were: you've enough to deck a maypole
As it is. Janet—your eyes . . . what's the matter?

JANET: There has been an accident, Mother.

MRS BRACE: I knew it—
The signs! O dear! O my poor Arthur!
[*collapsing into a chair*]

ROBERT [*caressing her*]: Now dearest, be brave.
We don't even know what has happened. Is it . . .?

JANET: Yes, I am afraid so. Mother, can you bear it?
Daddy—yes, he is dead.

MRS BRACE: Death by road! Tell me—
Wasn't it on the road?

PAUL: More or less, Mrs Brace.
He must have died at once, without any pain.

ROBERT: But how? Where?

JANET: In a car park not far from the factory.

ROBERT: That tells us nothing. Was he run over?

PAUL: It seems he was going to get into his car
And another car knocked him down—a wheel went over him.
That's what we think. We don't yet know the details.

ROBERT: Dad run over! I can't take it in.
Death couldn't happen to *him*—it's unthinkable.
He would have been prepared for it—taken steps beforehand,
Just as he always did.

MRS BRACE: Why didn't I trust them? I had it in my mind—
I spoke of it. Robert, you must have heard me say it:
Mercury subjects—that was your father—
Were warned against taking any journey by road
During this week? You remember I said it?

ROBERT: If you did, I took no notice of it, dearest. Those predictions
Are always so vague.

MRS BRACE: But now it has happened:
Death by road. O why did I not prevent him
From taking the car?

ROBERT: He would not have listened—
You know that. Dad always laughed at those forecasts.
He used to make them up for you, don't you remember?
Avoid decisions; Keep to your routine;
If you have red hair
You may find it profitable to stand on your head.
Poor old Dad. I can't bear to think of it—
[*he turns aside to weep*].

MRS BRACE: But *you* must never laugh at them again. For you see
They do tell the truth.

JANET: Does anyone, I wonder, really face the truth?
I need not have feared the shock for you, Mother,
I see you have cushioned it already.

MRS BRACE: What do you mean, dear?

JANET: O, I did it too. I think we all cushion it
One way or another. We ask about the circumstance

Of death, about when, and how, and where,
Because *those* belong to life; those are still a part
Of our known existence; we almost feel
As though we can *cure* death by learning all the facts.
We try to cancel, or control, what is uncontrollable.
But your way is simply an injection of falsehood—
Like the paralysing stuff that the spider injects
Into a living thing—you paralyse the fact
That might sting you; you desiccate it into a proof
Of all that nonsensical zodiac prophecy.
Death is not death any longer, but simply
A fortune-teller's trump card.

MRS BRACE: Janet, you are unkind to me.

JANET: I'm sorry, Mum. I did not mean to be.
It just came over me—here is something real
And we can't accept it for what it is.
O, my mind is in a whirl: I don't know what I feel.
I feel sorry for Daddy, and that's so foolish,
For life is not such a marvellous lot
After all; and then, besides that,
I feel as though I *ought* to be feeling something more.

ROBERT [*who has recovered*]: Janet, ma chérie, first you scold,
And then you become inconveniently honest.
No more analysis. You come with me.
Dearest, you sit there, and cry, if it helps you.
Janet and I will bring you some good strong tea.
[*Exit with* JANET.]

MRS BRACE: He's such a comfort. He should have been the girl,
And Janet would have been much happier as a boy.
Isn't it strange? But then I wanted a son.
Before she was born I did everything I could:
I drank bicarbonate and swallowed the right herbs,
I wore nothing but blue . . . Well, I didn't succeed,
But it must have done something to Janet. And then

A little while before she was born
I dreamt about a blue bird that choked me with its feathers.
That was strange, wasn't it? Poor lamb, she'll miss her father.
Although we didn't see much of him; his work
Took most of his time. Forgive my running on—
It *has* been a shock. And yet, do you know
Mr Squire, I feel as though I'd known it all the time.

PAUL: Really, Mrs Brace?

MRS BRACE: Of course, I'm psychic.
But why didn't I stop him, because of the signs?
I'll tell you what I think, Mr Squire: I think
This was *meant* to happen: I think I was held back
From speaking, by the Powers. Do you believe
In the Powers, Mr Squire?

PAUL: I don't know exactly:
I've never been certain about God, I'm afraid.
I write 'C of E' in the space marked Religion,
And that's about as far as I get. I must say
If there is a God, it is hard to imagine him
Reaching from the clouds to stop you from speaking
Like a—like a boy reaching into a pool
To stop up the mouths of the sea anemones.

MRS BRACE: It isn't that, at all. But we have to follow
What the Powers ordain for us, and if we do,
Then we are in tune—we live in harmony.

PAUL: If you mean that we can't change the course of events . . .

MRS BRACE: Our lives to be in tune—that is what matters.
Now, if you had chanced to be with my husband
To-day . . .

[*The door opens and* ROBERT *and* JANET *enter with tea.*]

PAUL: What do you mean, Mrs Brace?

ROBERT: Now
Tea for us all, with the tarry flavour,
The dash of extravagance. D'you know what I read
In a woman's weekly—a recipe for pancakes
With that Extra Something—guess what it was?
A spoonful of liver salts! Talk about extravagance
That seems to me an extravaganza.

JANET [*pouring out*]: And why were you *reading* a woman's weekly?
You pretend that you do it for something to laugh at,
But it can't be just that.

ROBERT [*aside to her*]: Keep talking, old girl:
Say anything you like; only keep talking.

PAUL: What could I possibly have done, Mrs Brace?

MRS BRACE: Don't look so alarmed—I am only imagining
If you had been there, and if you had been in tune
With the Powers, perhaps you might have pulled him aside.
If you had been there, you might have been sent
Just for that purpose; and if you had been there . . .

PAUL: Mrs Brace, why do you keep repeating that?
I was not there.

[*Telephone rings.*]

MRS BRACE: Answer that, Janet, please.
It was just an example
Of what I mean: of the way the Powers work.

JANET [*at telephone*]: Janet Brace speaking. Yes, Mr Brace's daughter.
Yes, we heard the news about an hour ago.
The inquest?
I hope we shan't any of us have to attend it.
What did you say? It *wasn't* an accident?
No, we heard nothing. . . . I don't believe a word of it.

This is some story that you're trying to work up.
No, the police haven't . . . What did you say?
It won't be the slightest use your coming. You can ring
Until Doomsday, I shan't come to open the door.
Good-bye. [*She slams the receiver down.*]

MRS BRACE *and* ROBERT: What is it? Who was it?

JANET: The *Midland Echo.*
Mr Squire, I don't understand it. They say
That Daddy . . . that it wasn't a straightforward accident.
'Injuries consistent with kicks and blows
From the feet'—that was the doctor's report
According to them. But they must be lying.
Didn't you say he was knocked down by a car?

PAUL: That is what they told me.

ROBERT: But you didn't see it happen?

PAUL: No, I didn't see it happen. I wasn't there.

MRS BRACE: He wasn't there. But I distinctly felt
There was Death in your aura, Mr Squire.

PAUL [*carefully*]: I explained to your daughter, Mrs Brace,
That I wasn't an eyewitness. All I know
Is what I was told at the factory.
I had gone back for overtime work
At about six o'clock, but no one was working.
There were lots of rumours. Then down came the Works Manager,
Said he was going to the Merry-Thought
To—identify the body. But there was no doubt,
And we had to send someone round to the family
To break the news gently; and would I go?

ROBERT: An accident, you said, but . . .

PAUL: Yes, it was an accident.

ROBERT: *How* did the car strike him?

PAUL: In the fog, I suppose.

JANET: I'm sure that's how it happened. Just as you said.
I think this is just a newspaper stunt.
A thing like that couldn't happen—not here,
In the middle of the town, and with people about.
Who would want to hurt Daddy, anyway? They said
He must have been—*trampled* to death. No.
It's just a scare story.

ROBERT: He might have had enemies
We didn't know of . . . But if he had died like that
The police would certainly have made some move.
They would have called, or telephoned.

MRS BRACE: Besides,
The signs warned against death *by road.*

[*The telephone rings. They all look at each other.*]

JANET: O dear.

ROBERT: Well, someone must answer it.

[*No one moves.*]

MRS BRACE: Janet dear—I can't.

JANET: O, I don't think I *can*, again.
Mr Squire—Paul—could you possibly? . . .

[PAUL *moves slowly to the telephone and picks up the receiver.*]

CURTAIN

ACT II

The Private Bar of the Merry-Thought. NELLO *behind bar.* JACK *standing with his pint;* ONLOOKER *at one of the two or three small tables, reading a newspaper.*

JACK: So what did you tell him?

NELLO: I tell him very little.
I pretend that my English is not at all good . . .

JACK: You wouldn't need to act like Sir Laurence Olivier
In order to do *that*—excuse my saying so.

NELLO: All right—you laugh, but I tell you this:
A lady comes into this bar for a drink
And she takes me for an Englishman.

JACK: Where was she from herself? From Honolulu?
Or was the bar in motion and hit her on the head?
Don't mind me, old chap—go on with what you were saying.

NELLO: Well, in any case the boss does most of the talking.
He tries to shut me up, and this detective
Tries to make me speak, and between them both
I feel like one of those dolls—*ventriloquio*—
What is the English word? I open my mouth,
But the sound is coming from someone else.

JACK: Did you mention me, or any of the boys?
It was mostly that crowd from the Roamers, you know.

NELLO: I have said that there were some from the factory.
If he wants to find out who, he will have to ask you all.
In any case, I only know that you are called Jack:
There are probably dozens of boys called Jack
At your factory, aren't there?

JACK: Then you did say my name?

NELLO: I do not think I did. I tell him very little.
The boss keeps on talking. But I have not told a lie
Like the gentleman over there.

JACK: Why, what did *he* say?

NELLO: He has said that he is not here at the time,
That he did not come in here yesterday at all.

JACK: And did he?

NELLO: He was sitting over there in the window
Just as he sits now. Every day he sits there.

ONLOOKER [*getting up and walking to bar*]: It is none of your business.
I don't know why you got mixed up in it yourself.
He treated you like a bit of your own macaroni.

NELLO: He was no worse than most of you are.
You English are not over friendly to foreigners.
Some call us Dagoes, and some remind us
Of battles when our countrymen ran away
Before we were born, perhaps.
Some call us Eyeties and won't let us work
Like your unions, Jack . . . . Well, what are you having, sir?

ONLOOKER: Another of the same, please.

NELLO: You make *me* tell a lie,
Or not tell what I know, and that does not like me.
If you wish to shut up your mouth like a . . . clam—
Well; but you cannot clamp for others.
Perhaps it ends that they clamp me in prison.
Anyway—the inquest is fixed for tomorrow:
I have to give evidence. [*To* JACK]
I do not think that you will be troubled.
But someone else was here with your boss:
A young chap. They eat together. After all is over
I look for him, but he is gone. He ought to give evidence.

[JANET *enters. She goes rather hesitantly to the bar, and* JACK *moves with his drink to a table.*]

JACK: Well, thanks a lot for the information.

JANET: I'd like a small sherry, please.

NELLO: Nice day, Miss, isn't it?
Specially after yesterday. There you are, Miss.

JANET: Thank you. Won't you have something with me?
A beer?

NELLO: That is very kind of you, Miss.

JANET: I suppose you were here all yesterday?

NELLO: Yes Miss, I was.

JANET: I heard—I read—that something happened here—
A car accident, was it?

NELLO: Well, in a way, Miss.

JANET: *Wasn't* it a car accident? The papers said so.

NELLO: It was to *do* with a car. Well, cheers, Miss.
Lovely day, isn't it?

JANET: Just the same
As when you last said so. Well, I must tell you:
I have a reason for asking you questions.
You must not put me off—this is too serious.
My father died here yesterday.

NELLO: It was your father, Signorina? O, I am sorry.

JANET: Yes. So I want you to tell me just what happened.

NELLO: Just what happened? What did they tell you happened?

JANET: I can't make sense of what I heard—that's why I've come.

NELLO: But will you tell me what you heard? That will help me.
I shall know where to begin.

JANET: I can't make sense of it.
First I heard—an accident. And there was a paragraph
In this morning's paper, which said just that.

Look [*showing it*]—'Well-known local industrialist knocked down by car'.
But then there is another story—something much more horrible:
Not an accident—a great wave of hatred
That swept him under. Was that what you saw?

NELLO: But who has told you that, Miss?

JANET: Trampled, they said.
I can't believe it.
In a revolution, such a thing might happen,
But not on an ordinary day, out of an ordinary sky,
Not to an innocent man—O, think of it!
For my father *was* innocent, surely? Except
In those things where all of us are guilty, who live.
You don't say anything,
O, won't you tell me what happened?

NELLO: Signorina, what you read in the papers might be true.
Better wait and see. Even if I tell you—
I tell it so badly—I am Italian—
I only distress you, confuse you . . .

JANET: I will risk that.
I must try to know the truth, for the sake of the dead.
We may be content with falsehoods for ourselves—
Half-truths—or we can cover what is painful
By talking of the weather, that all-blanketing bromide
Or wondering what's for dinner. But not for the dead.
Don't you see? They won't let us rest.
They know the truth—they are trying to tell us . . .

NELLO: Your father—he wasn't a Catholic, Miss?

JANET: Or perhaps it is we who will not let them rest.
Don't you think that might be so? While we are puzzling

And searching, our questions and cries must disturb them.
It is as though we haunted *them*:
We call them up—I have often thought that:
It was Hamlet himself who called the ghost of his father,
Although he didn't know it.
I'm sorry—you asked me if my father was a Catholic.
No, he was not.
I'm afraid he was not a religious man
In any kind of way. But he wasn't a coward;
And if he had done something bad—something
That brought about his death, he would want me to know it.
Won't you tell me?
Think that my father in me is asking you,
Begging you, so that I can come to understand
And leave him in peace. You could refuse me,
But you can't refuse a dead man.

NELLO: Cara Signorina—my dear Miss—you ask me
Something so difficult. It is so difficult
To tell you, and I do not understand it myself,
For the truth is horrible. And I promise Mr Colman—
My boss, that is—to say as little as I can:
Not to tell lies but—just that I answer questions
As shortly as I can. At the inquest, I mean.
But now . . .

JANET: I have a right to know. You have simply got to tell me.

JACK [*jumping up and going to bar*]: He has got to? Spoken with the boss's voice!
I knew your father, miss—at least, I worked for him;
He wouldn't have known *me*. I had nothing against him.
If he thought that our lives were moved by his conveyor belt

That was just because he was on top, and we weren't.
If he cooked the mechanism, so that the needle
Showed something less than the speed of the machine
As some chaps said he did—that was in the game.
Our chaps kept him on his toes, you can bet.
He had a good run for his money, with his Jag.
And his expense account; leave it at that.
I'm sorry it happened, but there it is.
Someone has switched him off at the main;
We can't start him up again. Better let it be, Miss.
Sudden death is sudden death: we all have to take
What's coming to us. Nello can't tell you any different.

JANET [*stunned, to* NELLO]: Is that what you think too?
Is that what I must take? I had thought there was more kindness
In ordinary people.

NELLO: Sit down, Signorina. I shall try to help you.
And you, Jack, since you have thrust in,
We shall both of us tell her what we can.
As to the meaning
I cannot help you. I have said it just now—
I do not understand what happened. But the cause
Why it happened—we must look at the beginning of the world
For that—or it may be, a word that we forget about,
We do not even mention it in our confession,
A word that we have spoken—it is like a tiny germ
Too small to be seen, that grows huge as Russia
And swallows us up.

JANET: Please tell me everything.
I shall try to bear it. But O, think what you say,
For your words throb through me, as though I were strung
To the pitch you sound.
He was here, in this room,
And you saw him, yesterday?

NELLO: Yes, he was here.

JANET: Can you show me? I want to imagine it all.

NELLO [*going to table*]: This is where he sits, and with him is a young chap
About the age of Jack, there. They are having tea
Because it isn't yet time for drinks.
I am here by the bar;
That gentleman [*pointing to* ONLOOKER] was there, just as he is now.
There is one other customer, finishing his tea.
He goes out, but soon he returns to say
That he wish to drive out, but your father's car
Is blocking the exit. [*A pause.*]

JANET: Yes? And what did Daddy say?

NELLO: The customer does not speak very politely.
Your father gets angry. He goes to the window,
Looks out, and says that there is plenty of room.
He goes back to his table, and calls for more hot water.
The customer is furious.
I think he is going to strike your father,
So I quickly say that I will come out and help him.
When we get there, we find that things are really nasty.
You know there was a League match yesterday afternoon?
Two of the coaches were parked in our yard.

JACK: The match hadn't gone too well; the referee
Got some bottles at his head, and he stopped the game.
The Roamers thought they should have had it in the bag,
So they came to their coaches in an ugly mood.

NELLO: Your father's car is blocking the way out
As I said, and the boys are all beating round it.
It is locked. If only the window has been open
Perhaps he would still be alive today.

I tell them that they must not touch it. I run
To the bar to fetch your father. At first he will not come,
Then he hears the noise . . .

JACK: A hell of a shindy . . .

NELLO: And he hurries out. But it is too late.
For by the time he comes they are forcing the door.
Now your father, he does not act wisely at all.
He ought to have talked to them quietly; instead
He shouts at them, calls them a bunch of bastards,
With other expressions. They cannot force the door.
I try to make them move, so that I can persuade him
To drive the car away. But he still shouts at them,
And suddenly a lot of them rush at the car
And start to push it over. Your father is knocked down
In the rush, and he cries for help. [*A pause.*]

JANET: And did no one try to save him? [*Another pause.*]

NELLO: I am waiting for these other gentlemen to speak.
That gentleman there was sitting in the window
And must have seen, and heard. But he will not speak.
If there had been several, we might have saved him,
But I was alone. The driver of the bus
And the other man had gone to fetch Mr Colman
Before the worst began. I try to pull him clear:
Some ten of them are shoving at the car, and others
Kick him as he lies on the ground.
[JANET *weeps.*] Signorina,
It is terrible, but you must not think
He felt it all, as you feel it, listening to me.

JANET: It's too horrible—and for you it must have been
Like the end of the world.

NELLO: Yes. But you see
It is over so quickly. I am trying madly
To get him away, and I have no time to think
Till afterwards. Now, I am in it all the day,
Trying to save him, and thinking backward,
Trying to alter what happened, if perhaps
I had spoken earlier, or done something different,
All would have been changed.

JANET: And did you not get hurt?

NELLO: A few kicks, but nothing much. I was frightened, though!
These boys, they are like a crowd at a bull-fight.
Then I see Jack, on the edge of it.

JACK: Miss,
I think all this would be better forgotten:
We can't alter it; we can't blame anyone. . . .

JANET: Not *blame*?

JACK: Well, not exactly: your father being
The kind of man he was, and the football crowd
Turning up just then.

JANET: And did you try to save him?
Did you help Nello?

NELLO: I call to him to help:
He seems to be—punch drunk; he doesn't move,
He doesn't seem to hear. What was wrong with you, Jack?

JACK: I sometimes had dreams—you won't like this, Miss Brace,
But you asked for the truth—they were day-dreams, I suppose.
I'd imagine the boss was sinking in the river,
And I was on the bank, with a rope. He would beg me
To save him, and at last I would throw him the line,

But not until he had gone under twice,
And begged me for mercy . . .
I'd taken the afternoon off for the match
And I came for my motor bike, left in the yard.
I saw it all begin: I didn't want to get mixed up,
But I couldn't get by. And then I thought—
They'll teach him a lesson: him and his posh car.
Then I heard him shout for help—I was back in my dream,
I couldn't move.

NELLO: Yet I think Jack would have helped me. After
I shouted, you were coming?

JACK: Yes, I heard you, and I saw
The blood run down his face, and I thought 'He can't see';
He had dirt in his mouth, too; I thought 'There are too many
Against one; I've had enough of this'; and I was going to help
When I heard a whistle, and someone yelled 'Police!',
And they all scarpered, and I ran too. [*Pause.*]
I didn't want to be caught—and how could I prove
That I wasn't in the fight?

JANET: You all ran off and left him
Lying there, all except Nello?

NELLO: Yes.
It isn't the police, but we are left alone,
And I say to him 'O, you will be all right now.'
I wrap my coat round him, and try to stop the blood,
But there is too much, and I think to try to carry him
Indoors, but then I see that his hurts are too bad.
I sit with his head on my knee; his eyes are closed;
They open for a flash, like a baby just born,
And his lips tremble with a word. He cannot speak it.

I try to commend his spirit to God.
I think he died then, but Mr Colman
Arrives with the others, and we carry him in.
We lay him down here, and we see that he is dead.
May his soul find peace.

JANET: Amen.
I am trying to take in what you are saying, but at present
I just can't see it. Please go on.

NELLO: Except for ourselves the bar is empty:
That gentleman there, and the other young fellow
They must have slipped away. Then the police arrive.
But before they come
Mr Colman says that he would like, if possible,
To let them think it was a car knocked him down.
He thought that if the papers told about the football crowd
And the kicking, that would be bad for our business.
That works all right at first. We send for the Works Manager
From Brace Electric for identification.
The late editions report it as an accident.
But afterwards, of course, there is the doctor's report,
And they question the coach driver. Today a detective
Was questioning me. Tomorrow at the inquest
I shall tell it just as I have told it to you.
Forgive me. It is hard to make you hear such things—
His daughter, and so young.

JANET: I should bless you for ever, for you showed mercy on him.
But O, I can't believe it. Such a tiny cause
For so vast a consequence as death! If he had harmed them—

But to die just for a blocked road and a few paltry swear-words—
It can't be. Search back—think again what happened.
Hadn't he some enemy there in that coach—
Someone who owed him a grudge? My father seemed a hard man
To some—you have said as much—but that is not enough,
Not to end in death. Oh, I cannot bear it
That he should die so terribly, and innocent!

NELLO: Signorina,
You would not have us find out a crime for him, surely?

JANET: But to put some *reason* in it.

JACK: How I look at it,
You're punished for what you are. You may do things
In your life that you might deserve to hang for
And go scot free, but sooner or later
The punishment comes—it catches up with you.

NELLO: The cruelty, that is a dreadful thing,
Something far worse than the cruelty of animals.
Men cannot behave like beasts, because they are still men.
These boys betrayed us all. But for the cause of death,
That it should be so small, which torments you so,
Perhaps you forget that we are all under sentence.
Think of this, for instance.
My sister had a boy—the joy of her heart:
One day she gave him his gloves and his cap;
He was to go sliding with the others on a pond—
Not a very big one, not far away.
Well—the ice broke under him. Gone in a flash,
His jokes, his joy, and the toil that went to raise him,

Vanished under the water. And still, day and night,
She hears him call her name, from the torrent his torment,
With no one to answer him. Where was the sense of it?
Where was the cause? Just for ten minutes
Play on a pond. Signorina, such a thin ice
Separates us all from drowning! We forget it
Because God is kind, but . . .

ONLOOKER: Because God is kind?
How can you say that?

JACK: He has found his tongue at last!

ONLOOKER: You cannot have eyes in your head or a heart under your ribs
If you say that God is kind. Kindness? Why
There is not even justice.
'Whatever brute or blackguard made the world . . .'
As Housman put it—I wasn't very old
When I learnt the truth of that.

NELLO: But it is man's fault—we make our own suffering.

JANET: O Nello—and the ice on the pond—was that our fault?

NELLO: The Church tells me so. I don't pretend to understand it.

ONLOOKER: Tch—original sin, and all that poppycock.
Well, it's not my business if you like to believe in fairies.

JANET: You watched my father die, and that was not your business?

ONLOOKER: Young lady, no, it was not. For you it is regrettable
No doubt, to lose a father in such a sordid way.
For him—well, it was a quick death.

JANET: There is a cruelty in talking like that
Which is just as appalling as if you had joined in
And kicked him as he lay.

ONLOOKER: I am sorry for you.
And yet I suppose that it will do you no harm
To learn what other girls have to learn when they are children.
Haven't you lived an easy life? Ate when you were hungry?
Retired at night to a dimity white bed
In your own little room? If you had grown as I did
With birth and intercourse and death going on
Within the four walls where you lived, you'd have learnt
Not to poke your nose in where you were not asked to.
You'd have soon learnt to mind your own business.
Yesterday's business was nothing to do with me.
What call did I have to mix myself up
In a fight over a car park?

JANET: None. None at all—
Unless you were a human being.

ONLOOKER: Say, a Dago:
That's how your father would've described this barman
Who did interfere.
But I've made you angry:
You should thank me for that.
I have given you an obvious target for your anger.
Anger warms the heart, and takes away the chill
Of the cold steel of truth. It's so unsatisfying
To be angry with Fate.

JANET: You are wrong.
I could feel anger at what you have said
And because you did nothing, if I were at leisure
To feel anything about you at all: but I am not.
I am trying to reconcile my father's death
With his life—to see the seed of one in the other—

O, to make some sense of it! I know this, at least:
That from his blood sprang a whole azalea of charity—
It was not all degradation. Nello,
That is from you. The crowd that killed him—
I hope I never know who they were: it is better
To think of them as faceless—the ice on the pond,
The cruel water. Or soulless, like you [*to* ONLOOKER]
Who watch as though life were a television screen.
That other man who was there—I don't want to know
Who *he* was either.
And you [*to* JACK] have given me something to think of:
Something to forgive— O yes—but also
Something to understand—to see that my father
Whom I loved, seemed almost an enemy to you.
I had better go now.
I shall have to explain it to my mother, somehow,
And my brother—somehow we must live with the truth.
Good-bye, Nello. I shall never forget you.

NELLO: Good-bye, Signorina. [*Opening door.*] If only I could have saved him,
But . . . [*Exit* JANET.]
The poor, poor girl!
If only her father had not come here yesterday,
If only . . . but it's just madness to try to change the past.
I keep turning it about in my mind
Like the pieces of a puzzle, trying to make it
Show me something different. I wish I could stop.

JACK: Well, you do that, old chap:
Forget the whole thing. That's what I shall do—
Forget that I ever came near this place yesterday.

NELLO: Tell me, did you recognize any of the boys
In that crowd, would you know them again?

JACK: If I did—
And I'm not saying I did—I shouldn't let on.
Not me.

NELLO: But you ought to, you know.
I couldn't identify anyone myself,
But if there were some that you know . . .

JACK: None of that.
No names, no pack-drill, that's my motto.
You won't catch me giving evidence. Too risky:
You never know who you might offend. Besides
I wasn't here yesterday. Just remember that.
I must be going. There's a scramble on to-morrow—
Got to get the bike oiled. So long. [*Exit.*]

NELLO [*to* ONLOOKER]: But you at least,
You will confirm what I tell of the accident?

ONLOOKER: I don't expect I shall.
Not unless you make me. Of course you could do that—
You realize? But you are far too good-natured;
I'm relying on that. I'll be getting on too.

[*As he is going out, he meets* PAUL *entering.*]

Why, here's the other man. Maybe he will help you.

[*Exit.* PAUL *goes to the bar, but says nothing.*]

NELLO [*after a pause*]: What can I get you, sir?

PAUL: I must know, did you tell her?

NELLO: Tell her? Whom do you mean, sir?

PAUL: You know—Miss Brace. She was here just now.
She said she would be coming. I watched until she left,
And then I had to see you, to find out. O
The torments that I have been through, since yesterday!

NELLO: Because you ran away, sir?

PAUL: Partly because of that,
But also—tell me first, what does she know?

NELLO: I have told her everything.

PAUL: O God, then she knows!

NELLO: Of her father's terrible death, yes, she had to find it out.
Would you have had me refuse to tell her?
She asked for the truth.

PAUL: No, it had to be faced
Since the police discovered it. But need you have told her
That I was here, too?

NELLO: How can I do that
When I do not know myself who you were? I only tell her
Someone is with her father: someone who . . . ran away
As I suppose, when the trouble began:
Or what should I call it?

PAUL: Call it what you like
If *she* doesn't know it. What about the inquest?
Look here: I'll give you anything I can
If you keep my secret. I haven't much money, but . . .
How much would you want?

NELLO: I suppose I ought to knock you down.
First you run away, and then you insult me.
But you are very young and very silly. I prefer
To ask you why you act as you did. This man
Was your employer, wasn't he? When you have seen what happened
And have heard him shout for help, why do you do nothing?

PAUL: I still don't really know. Give me something to drink
And I'll try to tell you.
That scene! I've been acting it
Ever since yesterday—even in my sleep I think,
And all the while that people were talking.
It's a moving stair that I have to travel
From the bottom to the top, and at the top
I am back at the beginning. A hell-go-round . . .

NELLO: A hell-go-round. I know it too well:
I am doing it too.

PAUL: But you have no reason:
You did what you could.
Why should you rehearse it in your mind?

NELLO: Why
To make it end differently! To go into that yard
And do something that would stop it.

PAUL: One never knows
How one will act, at the test. You won't have played Rugger,
So you don't know what it feels like, at the bottom of the scrum.
When I have nightmares, that's where I am,
With boots in my mouth, not able to breathe.

NELLO [*as he pauses*]: So you looked through the window?

PAUL: It wasn't *just* funk.
Or perhaps it was. But I was feeling sore:
I wasn't making a success of my job,
My first, and he didn't understand how I felt,
Didn't try to understand: he simply told me
To put some cotton-wool in my ears, and snap out of it.
'What did you expect?' he said. 'A nursery garden?
I'm not going to put you under a cloche.'
When I tried to explain, he just shouted me down.

NELLO: I heard a bit of that.

PAUL: So when I looked out
And saw there was a row, I thought 'Snap out of it—
You told me to do that—and that's just what I'll do.'

NELLO: But how much did you see?

PAUL: I saw them crowding round, and you trying to disperse them;
I thought that his car might get damaged, and that he
Might get a few bruises . . .

NELLO: And was that all?

PAUL: God, no! Why should I pretend?
I knew I ought to go, and I heard that sort of growl
Like a beast in a cage, and felt the crowd on top of me,
And I was in a panic.
That chap in the window
Just sat there smoking, and said 'It looks nasty:
Someone might get hurt, if they aren't more careful.
It's your boss, isn't it?' He gave a sort of smile,
And he looked at me as if he knew what I was feeling.
'Aren't you going to help him?' 'I'll go for the police'
I said. 'Someone's done that, I expect', he answered.
'But by the time they get here . . .' I thought, 'I must do something.'
And I ran out by the front, away from the yard
And that awful snarling. I couldn't see a bobby
So I ran on, up the road. At last I saw one, running,
And I followed to be sure that he was making for the yard,
And he was. So I thought—I hoped—
He would get there in time.

NELLO: Then you didn't hear your boss shout for help?

PAUL: No, did he?
It would take a lot to make him do that.
If I had heard him call, perhaps I might have gone—
I don't know—I should like to think so.
But when I was outside, and I saw the bobby running,
I thought the best thing was to get right away.
I thought the police would soon put things straight,
And the best thing for me was to know nothing about it—
So I went back to work.
Then I heard that he was dead—
Hit by a car, they thought. Well, it just might have been true:
I convinced myself of that. They sent me to his home
To break the news to his family.

NELLO: Yes?

PAUL: Well, what could I do? What would you have done?
I told them what I had heard. I almost
Persuaded myself that I was telling them the truth.
God, I could kill myself!

NELLO: What use would that be?
You have lost the picture of yourself that you like—
The one that we all like—the picture on the front
Of the cornflakes packet, all smiles and crackle.
But it was never true. No one was ever
So rosy and innocent as that. O no.
Now you have seen yourself a coward and a liar.
Well—it's a good start.

PAUL: You think so?
You have a queer notion of a good start in life!
Besides, there's something else—something more than the loss
Of the cornflakes picture. That girl who was here—

He was her father!
O why didn't I know that last week? What cruel fate
Delayed our meeting until just the moment
When to know her was despair?

NELLO: Despair and Fate—
Those are grand words, I think. Coward and liar—
Those aren't grand at all . . .
Shall I see you at the inquest?

PAUL: Good heavens, no. Why should I do that?

NELLO: They have asked for witnesses. As you were there . . .

PAUL: But what good would it do?

NELLO: Perhaps only
To yourself, though it might help me, just a little,
Since you were another witness. But mostly for yourself.
You need the dead man's forgiveness, don't you?

PAUL: His forgiveness? It is hers I want.

NELLO: It is his you need. Hers too, but that is different.

PAUL: If I thought that it would help her . . . but no, it can't help,
And whatever I do, this death must lie between us
For ever, I can never hope to make her my wife.
Let me at least leave a good thought behind me.

NELLO: A good thought—that is false?

[*Enter* DETECTIVE.]

DETECTIVE: Sorry to bother you once again:
There are just a few questions I wanted to ask.
This young fellow who had tea with the deceased—
Can you give me a description?

[NELLO *is confused and does not answer*.]

PAUL: [*laughing*] Why, Nello, as you described him to me, he sounded
The image of myself!

DETECTIVE [*to* NELLO]: Is that so? Well, that is very convenient, isn't it?

[*Looking at* PAUL *and writing.*]

Hair (*). Height (*).
But we might as well be accurate: what *is* your height, sir?

PAUL: (*), I believe.

DETECTIVE: Age, early twenties? But if I may say so
An Identi-kit from this might suit a good many.
The police would prefer him with warts, or a birth-mark!

[*to* NELLO]

Had he any special distinguishing mark
That you can recall?

NELLO: Er—no, I don't think so.

DETECTIVE: And you didn't know his name?
Hadn't seen him before?

NELLO: That is correct, sir.

DETECTIVE: Odd that he hasn't come forward, don't you think so?
Well, good day to you.

PAUL: Why do you want to find him?
I thought Nello said he had nothing to do with it—
Left before the row began?

NELLO: I don't know that.
I didn't see him go.

DETECTIVE: We shall soon find out.
It shouldn't be difficult to track him down
If he came from the factory. Thanks for the help.

[*Exit.*]

PAUL: Name—Poor Bloody Es-Squire. Age—Born Yesterday.
Distinguishing Mark—why didn't you say it?
He's yellow all through.
Destination?—

*Fill in according to actor's description

NELLO: He can choose it.
Finish up your drink: I'm going to close now.

[PAUL *drains his glass and begins to move towards the door.*]

PAUL: Nello, if I had gone out to help you,
I couldn't have prevented what happened, could I?

NELLO: I cannot say. It might be that together
We could have done something. Or perhaps not.
You will never be sure of that, I am afraid.
You will tell yourself that you could have done nothing,
But . . .

PAUL: I shan't convince myself. No, I shan't convince myself . . .
For the rest of my life . . .

CURTAIN

ACT III

The Braces' sitting-room. JANET *and her mother.* MRS BRACE *is mending,* JANET *wandering round the room.*

MRS BRACE: Janet, dear, I wish you would sit down.
You make me nervous, wandering about
Like a bird whose nest has been moved, or a cabbage-white
Looking for a cabbage. Find something to do.
Why don't you darn your stockings, instead
Of throwing them away, or patch this coat of Robert's?
He won't be back from the inquest yet,
So you'd much better settle to something.

JANET: I suppose so.
Give me the coat, then. I can't really think
Until we know the verdict. Yet what difference can it make?
Nothing can take away the horror that happened.
I suppose that in my heart of hearts I don't think it's true—
I'm hoping for some new fact to make it all different.

MRS BRACE: You do think that barman was telling you the truth?

JANET: Why should he not? What do you mean?

MRS BRACE: I cannot understand how the signs could lie.
It was such a clear case of Death by Road.

JANET: And now that you can't predict what happened, backwards,
The universe is out of control again!

MRS BRACE: You have taken the scissors. Yes, it was quite clear—
Except for Paul Squire.

JANET: You keep saying that: 'Death in his face'.
I think it is absolutely idiotic.

MRS BRACE: Perhaps I mistook it.
Perhaps it was a marriage, not Death, that I saw.
I wonder. Of course he's much too young,
But the signs would favour it: you are both Aquarius . . .

JANET: Don't talk nonsense, Mother. Keep the wool for the socks
And don't spin it into webs. I like Paul Squire,
But I'm not in the habit of falling in love
With everyone I like.

MRS BRACE: O, you despise my intuition,
But it gets me farther in important directions
Than all your logic. 'Do be reasonable'
You say. But Life is not a column of figures,
It's X, the unknown quantity. O, your poor father,
If I could only have persuaded him of that
He might be here today.

JANET: And would you be glad of that?

MRS BRACE: Janet, you sometimes show a flash or two
In spite of your literal mind. But—yes and no.
It wasn't all roses, living with your father.
I got the smaller share of him: the bigger part
Was always swallowed by his work. I shared him
With joints and switches and sockets and so forth.

JANET: To be jealous of a female-plug! That's not very flattering,
You poor dear. And yet perhaps it doesn't hurt as badly
As jealousy of women; and you had such different tastes.
If you had seen too much of each other
It wouldn't have worked.

MRS BRACE: I was a good wife to him.
He always had a clean shirt and a clean pocket-handkerchief
And the food that suited him; it wasn't my fault
If he lacked imagination.

ANET: An odd word to use
For those star-gazing, card-shuffling fancies of yours.

MRS BRACE: Now Janet, I won't have that . . .

JANET: No, don't let's quarrel.
I imagine it was partly Father's fault
That you got so obsessed with those magazines:
This Old Moore's Almanac kind of existence—
Everything reduced to an astrologer's column
In a woman's weekly—all turquoises and tea-leaves.

[*She takes up the photograph of* BRACE.]

But then, somewhere that part of him got lost.
How did that happen? Was it there when you married him?

MRS BRACE: It was always there, my dear, if you had had eyes for it.
I knew it—O yes, you thought me stupid,
Not his intellectual equal—you were to take that place.
But the soul you see there—that was for me;
I could always find it. I suppose it was for that
I married him: it wasn't for want of other offers.
Of course we were compatible too—both of us Aries.
We were a handsome pair: our wedding picture
Was kept in the photographer's window for months.
Ah well—he lost his looks with his hair.
Poor dear; but I still have something of mine.
Perhaps I shall marry again: my horoscope
Says I am meant for a creative force,
But only in marriage. I *feel* that to be true.
I'm sure that I couldn't look to you for comfort
In my old age; you will go your own way
As you have always done.

JANET: O Mother, am I really
So hard and unfeeling? It's difficult for anyone
To understand another person, and for us
So different as we are, more difficult than ever.
I should like to try, now that you are alone.
Don't take another husband, I'm sure he would be awful.
I'll wait till next year to start my training—
That won't be too late. We'll go abroad together.
With lots to see and do, you won't have the time
For all that star-scrappery. We could learn together,
Go to picture-galleries. . . .
I'd love to travel—I feel I hate England
Just now . . . with this horror. We'll make a fresh start.
Don't you like the idea?

MRS BRACE: Why, child, we should quarrel in a month—in a week.
I wouldn't mind a holiday in the South of France
And wear my new sun-suit . . . But I don't want to study:
At my time of life I have learnt what I like
And that's enough for me. But Robert—that's difficult.
He won't like a stepfather.

JANET: Robert is the one
Who would profit by the change. Now I come to think of it,
You unmarried would never let him go.
Yes, it would be better for him if you did marry.
Only, do be careful. Don't pick some frightful man
Just because he was born under the right sign of the Zodiac.
And remember, too, you can't have it both ways:
You can't reproach me as an unfilial daughter
If you won't even try my suggestion.

MRS BRACE: Your suggestion!
I wonder what you would do if I actually accepted it.

How little you understand of Life—or of yourself, child.
We were speaking of Paul Squire, now . . .

[*A ring at the bell.*]

That must be Robert—he's forgotten his key as usual.
Go and let him in, dear—Inge's gone shopping.
Or else it was folk-dancing.

JANET: Also as usual! [*She goes out and returns with* PAUL.]
It's Paul Squire, Mother.
Do sit down, Paul—I'll go and get some tea.
Or would you prefer coffee, as it's early yet for tea?

PAUL: Neither, thank you, and I won't sit down
If you don't mind. I have something to say
That is better told standing. Like a prisoner in the dock,
For that is what I am.

MRS BRACE: You knew something
About my husband's death—something you didn't tell us?

PAUL: Yes, Mrs Brace.

MRS BRACE: I knew it! You see, Janet?
Always trust your instinct. You had something to do with it?

PAUL: Not exactly that:
But I did know about it; at least . . .

JANET: Paul
I don't understand you. You were nowhere near:
You said so. You didn't even know what really happened
Until that newspaper rang us up.
You were as horrified at that as we were.
What do you mean?

PAUL: It is like a death
To stand here and tell you, but that's why I have come,
To suffer now what I should have suffered then.

And because—I don't know how to explain it—
I am so far off from you, a universe away:
While you don't know the truth, I am cut off
Even more than if you hated me—as you *will* hate me
When you know . . .

JANET: Well, go on, we are waiting.

PAUL: Yes,
I was there on Thursday, before they killed your father;
I was the man who was with him in the bar.

JANET [*still incredulous*]: But you said . . .

PAUL: Yes, I know: I couldn't tell you,
Not then. I didn't know for certain what had happened,
And then I hoped you need never know
That I had been near at the time. I didn't realize
How to deceive you would banish me for ever
From even the thought of you. Now you must loathe me,
But I—at least I can think of you again.
I am in your mind as myself, and not a dummy—
A virtuous dummy who never existed.

JANET: But you haven't told us anything. You say you were *there*.
And you didn't go to help him?

MRS BRACE: Or did Mr Squire
Perhaps join in?

PAUL: O no, no, not that!
I didn't see it all: only the beginning.
I didn't think anything like *that* would happen.
At least—no—I must make myself face it:
I tried to think afterwards he might have got away,
But at the time, you see, I was terrified—
Terrified. Do you know what it is
To feel terror at people who have gone completely mad?

If you had heard them snarling . . . and I felt so helpless:
What could I do? I stood there frozen,
And then I did run for the police.
Well,
Thank God you know it now!

MRS BRACE: I suppose you have told them all this at the inquest?

PAUL: No, I wanted you to hear it first,
And from me. O, I have suffered torments
Since yesterday, wondering how I could tell you,
Wishing to, fearing to . . .

JANET: Is that what you think of?
Your suffering, *your* fear? What must *he* have felt?
Perhaps you could have saved him, if you had gone out
When Nello did. But then of course you *might* have got hurt. . . .
Something *might* have happened to your precious skin.

PAUL: You can say what you like: you have a right to.
I have said I was terrified. But at the first moment
There was another reason. Let me try to explain.

JANET: There is no need to.
You owed my father nothing—he was only a man.
I am his daughter. Why should you wish
To justify yourself to me? Don't trouble to.
There's really nothing more for us to say to each other:
You had better keep the rest of the tale for the police.

PAUL: Of course you are right: there is no justification.
One reason is simply as bad as another.
God! if I had been as old on Thursday
As I am now, I could have done something.
It seems to me that I was just a child, then.

I know now that merely to be in the world
Makes you responsible, even for something
You did not begin, and for someone you've no love for.
I'll go now; but when you think of me
And condemn, as you must, remember just this:
I condemn my own self more bitterly than you can—
I have lost faith in myself; and I have lost you.
Good-bye. [*Turning at door.*] O, but—one word more:
It is very doubtful if I *could* have saved him.
You did not see that crowd.

JANET: We shall never know that.
We shall never know what *might* have happened.

[*Enter* ROBERT *with* NELLO.]

ROBERT: Well, here I am. More glimpses of the obvious.
O, hullo, Squire.
This is Nello, Mother, from the Merry-Thought.
Janet—I think you've met. Paul Squire—Nello Rossi.
You know what he did, Mum, and I've brought him home
So that you can thank him.

MRS BRACE [*holding out both hands*]: And I do thank him
From the bottom of my soul.

NELLO: It was nothing, Signora.
I only wish . . .

MRS BRACE: That you could have saved him? Ah
It was fated otherwise. The great Wheel of Fate
Turns whether we will or not.

JANET: But what was the verdict?
Did they get the ringleaders? or—anyone?

ROBERT: The verdict was manslaughter, not murder,
Against persons still unknown.
Whether the police will take the matter further
Is anyone's guess. But I hope they do.

MRS BRACE: My poor boy, you're looking so tired.
Come and sit down.
You must be half dead with the strain of it all.

ROBERT: No, Mother—I have to make a confession.
Although of course it was ghastly in a way,
I half enjoyed it: it was so dramatic,
And I could see people pointing me out,
'That's his son', and I tried to look solemn,
But I couldn't persuade myself it was real.
It's like seeing Venice after all the picture postcards:
I've met the kind of thing so often on the screen
Or in plays, I couldn't believe it was myself,
And my own father.

MRS BRACE: Picture postcards of Venice?
Really Robert, that is not in good taste.

ROBERT: O Mum, don't you see what I mean?

JANET: He likes acting,
He ought to be going on the stage. But Nello,
Did anyone give evidence besides yourself?

NELLO: First there is my boss, Mr Colman, and then
The driver of the coach. But you see, the trouble is, Miss,
There were so many of them pushing at the car,
It was all so confused—no one can tell.
I couldn't be sure to recognize anyone
Who actually touched your father. Not for certain.

ROBERT: I bet you could recognize some of them, at least.
I wish you would: I want to see them punished.

JANET: And the—other people who were there in the bar:
They didn't dare to appear, I suppose?

NELLO [*looking uneasily at* PAUL]:
It was a surprise, Signorina: that man
Who spoke so rudely to you—who had watched
From the window—he came along to give evidence.

ROBERT: He came just to see if anyone appeared
To back up Nello, and as no one did
He gave evidence himself. Said he was a fool
For doing it, but then, he had always liked Italians.

NELLO: The boy called Jack didn't come, you see . . .

JANET: And the man who was seen in the bar with my father?

ROBERT: They haven't found him yet. He was a swine
To stand by and do nothing. I hope they do get him.

JANET: Though what could they do? He wasn't *involved*,
Was he?

PAUL: Mr Brace—I am the man.

ROBERT: You!

PAUL: Yes.
I came to tell your sister—and your mother—to-day.
I shall go to the police next.

ROBERT: The police! They can't touch you,
As Janet says. You wretched canary!
You just ran away. You've the pith of a banana.
Why do we let him stay here? Why don't we tell him to get out?
I can't reach the others, so I'll hand this to you
As their representative. [*He hits* PAUL *in the face.*]

JANET [*as he does so*]: Don't, Robert.

PAUL: I'll take it. I deserve it.

MRS BRACE: Sit down, Mr Squire. You are not much hurt?

PAUL [*handkerchief to face*]: Thank you, it's nothing.

MRS BRACE: It's bleeding badly. I'll fetch some cold water.
Keep quite still.

JANET: You shouldn't have done that, Robert. It's degrading,

And I see now how useless it is
To want people punished: it's utterly irrelevant.
It can't help the dead.

ROBERT: How do you know that?
Ghosts have returned to ask for vengeance.
What about Hamlet's father? He couldn't rest in peace
Until he was revenged.

JANET: But revenged on whom? This is not Denmark.
O, what makes this so bewildering to me
Is that no one quite meant it to happen—it came
Not from a flame of evil, but just a cold *not caring;*
Kicking a man like a leaking sandbag
As though his life were no more than a flicker
In a horror film. Nobody cared but Nello.
If you punished anyone, you would have to take them all
And imprison them just for being what they were,
Or for not *being* at all. O Nello, what is wrong with us?
Why aren't we alive?

[MRS BRACE *returns as* JANET *is speaking, and busies herself with* PAUL.]

NELLO: Signorina
I have never had to answer such a question.
At Rocco di Papa, a slum near Rome
Where I grew up—on bread and pennies from tourists—
We never doubted that we were alive,
Even when our stomachs held nothing but air
And our heads nothing but thoughts of food.
The priest had bread—it was the body of Jesus
And ours too. The tourists had much more than bread,
And that was not ours. Between those two facts
Which we learnt early, there were many questions
But not the one you ask me. There, the winter wind

Comes straight off the snow, and the violets are sometimes late
That earn us our pennies, but still we do not doubt
That we are alive.

MRS BRACE: Of course you do not.
Janet is overwrought, to ask such a foolish question.

ROBERT: Janet has had breakfast and lunch, or she would not ask it.
We are alive, but *he* has had his life taken from him,
And who is to pay for that? [*Front door bell rings.*]
O damn that bell,
Who can it be now? [*Exit.*]

JANET: It is not revenge that the dead are asking.
I feel now what it is—I feel him stirring,
Circling about me, a feverish spirit
Nagging me to speak.

MRS BRACE: You *are* overwrought, dear.
Come and lie down.

PAUL: What is he saying? I don't deserve to know,
But have pity, and tell me. . . .

[*Re-enter* ROBERT, *with the* DETECTIVE.]

ROBERT: Inspector Johns, from the C.I.D.
My mother, Inspector; and this is my sister.
Mr Rossi you know. And this is . . .
O, I should explain,
I have just hit Mr Squire in the face, Inspector.

DETECTIVE: Indeed!

ROBERT: You were going to ask us something about him,
But now he can tell you himself.

PAUL [*rising*]: Yes.
I was coming to you myself. I am sorry you have forestalled me.

DETECTIVE: Well, Mr Squire, you'd have saved us some trouble
If you had done that earlier. But never mind that now.

I understand that you were with the deceased
Just before his death. I shall want you to tell me
Everything you said to each other. But first—
Did you recognize any in the crowd that killed him?

PAUL: Before I answer that, could I ask Miss Brace a question?

DETECTIVE: Well—yes, if you wish.

PAUL: Miss Brace, you said just now
That you felt as though your father were trying to tell you something. . . .

JANET: I can hear it still. It is—it is something
I do not want to hear, but I know that I must.
Robert, I think when you struck that blow
You struck it at *him*. The word I can hear
And do not want to hear—it is that we should pardon:
That we should speak the word which *he* cannot speak.
He could never rest in peace, with that unsaid word
A stone at his heart.

[DETECTIVE, *embarrassed, clears his throat.*]

MRS BRACE: Do sit down, Inspector.
My daughter is psychic, like me, although at present
I don't quite understand her.

ROBERT: But how can we forgive for the dead?

JANET: Nello,
You understand me?

NELLO: The dead are not bound
Either to the wrongs or the sorrows they knew here,
They are free. You mean that we should not claw them back
With thinking of their injuries—reliving their deaths? . . .

ROBERT: But my father was not a forgiving sort of man.
Just, but not forgiving.
He would more likely have wished us to punish
His murderers—we have no right to make an amnesty.

DETECTIVE: And you forget, Miss Brace, that the law must take its course.
If Mr Squire can identify anyone
It is his duty to tell us. He has also
To account for his own movements. The law knows no amnesty.

JANET: But we are not bound to behave as the law behaves.
Heaven forbid we should get our own justice.
An amnesty—that means a forgetting:
The drink of the dead, that sets them free
From the memory of evil.
O I wish I could drink that dark nectar.
It is true what you say, Robert: he was not one to forgive;
He thought it not rational, perhaps: a wrong
Should be paid for. But now we inherit his estate
And his injury with it. I think he has bequeathed us
The right to make an amnesty.

ROBERT: To set him free. . . .
But wait a bit—Father wasn't ready to die.
I should say his soul was a tiny seedling:
It couldn't have been much bigger than mine.
He wasn't even given the time to water it.

NELLO: We do not know that. The moment of death
Is a long one. I remember that look of his
Like a new-born child. Perhaps it *was* a new birth.

JANET: I told you, Paul, do you remember,
That there might be time for aeons of pain
In the moment of death? Then there might be time
For aeons of repentance and fresh resolve.

PAUL: A fresh start . . . is such a thing possible?

MRS BRACE: You cannot annul the past, Mr Squire
If that is what you mean. It is all written down
In the Book of Life.

DETECTIVE: Forgive me, Miss Brace:
It is not just punishment the law is concerned with,
But also with prevention. If we can catch some
From that crowd, we may make them an example
to the rest.

PAUL: They were mostly men from another town
Who had come in the coach. A few from our
factory
Were there in the yard, but I didn't see them
joining in.

DETECTIVE: Well, you can tell us what you know. We shall try
you
With a few of their faces.

PAUL: I'll tell you what I can.

DETECTIVE: And Mr Rossi. Sorry to trouble you again,
But we may need you for this further enquiry.

MRS BRACE: You must have something first. Robert, find Inge—
I think she must be back—ask her to get the tea.

ROBERT [*going to door*]: I'll see what I can do. But it's folk-dance
Friday
And Inge is sure to be gathering Peascods. [*Exit.*]

DETECTIVE: You know, Mrs Brace, I think we should get back
To the station pretty soon, if these gentlemen are
ready.

MRS BRACE: Inspector, a thought has just struck me. Tell me—
What day is your birthday?

DETECTIVE: I had the misfortune
To be born on a quarter day—the 25th of March.

MRS BRACE: Somehow I knew it! You must come with me at
once
To my star-chamber, and let me cast your horoscope.
I shan't let you leave this house till it is done.

DETECTIVE: But Mrs Brace, I really . . .

MRS BRACE: Would it surprise you to learn
That the day of your birth is the same as my late husband's?
The identical day. There is a strange conjunction
And we leave these things unexplored at our peril.
Come with me. Mr Rossi—I may need your help.
But first I must see the Inspector privately.

DETECTIVE: But my dear lady, I really haven't time . . .

MRS BRACE: Mr Squire—I am sorry if I spoke to you harshly:
You must try to get in tune—in tune with the Powers. . . .
That is what we all need. Now, come with me, Inspector. [*He looks helplessly at* JANET.]

JANET: Could you, just for a moment?

DETECTIVE: Well, dear lady,
If it will please you. . . . Just for five minutes, then.

[*Exeunt.*]

JANET: You see that my mother is quicker to forgive
Than either of her children!

PAUL: If there were anything I could do for you . . .
If it would ease the pain at your heart
To hate me, I would say anything—but no,
I mustn't seek the luxury of making you hate me
Instead of despising me. I'll try to take it honestly:
To swallow the cold remains of yesterday's failure,
And then, just to kneel on the solid ground
And ask your pardon, Janet.

JANET: O get up, get up, I don't like you to do that.
Not to me—to Nello, you might, but not to me.
In any case, I need pardon rather than to give it.
I should have been your advocate, to get your freedom,
And instead I made myself the judge, the prosecution
And the jury—the hanging jury—all at once.

It was not just for my father—you will have guessed that:
I could not bear to know that you had acted as a coward
And lied to me.

PAUL: I lied at first to a stranger,
And when I knew you, it was too late.
I would sooner have knelt to adore you
Than to ask your pardon. But those are words
I must not speak now. Perhaps never?

JANET: Never, Paul?
Both now and never seem a great way off:
Out of my sight, at least.

PAUL: Can one ever start afresh?

NELLO: An amnesty, the signorina said.
I think there is a kind of balance here:
The dead man cannot speak, but you speak for him
Signorina; and those who killed him do not speak,
Their debt falls upon you. [*To* PAUL.]

PAUL: A lifetime will not pay it, but all that I am
I give to that repentance.
Good-bye, Janet.

[*Enter* ROBERT.]

ROBERT: Nello, the Inspector implores you to come.
Mother thinks that his destiny is intertwined with hers—
He is terrified! She is still consulting the stars
And plotting his horoscope. He escaped to the hall
To try to find his coat—then Inge appeared
And tried to make him go down to the cellar
To look at the meter. He thinks he's in Bedlam!
He wants you to go with him at once.

NELLO: Then good-bye, Signorina.

JANET: Good-bye, Nello.
Good-bye, Paul. [PAUL *cannot speak, but looks at her, and then at* ROBERT *as he goes out.*]

ROBERT [*coming down stage*]: Poor Inge! I've laughed at her so much over this
That next time the gas-man comes he will find
The cellar door locked and barred in his face.
[*Seeing* JANET'S *tears.*]
I'm sorry, old girl. I did do my best
When I saw what you wanted. I find it very hard
To forgive them myself. And yet I didn't love Dad
Half as much as you did. I haven't your charity.
Perhaps I'm glad I haven't: it only makes you suffer.

JANET: Tomorrow starts again as though nothing had happened.
Life seems very long, when it stretches ahead of you.

ROBERT: And wide, wide! There is so much to enjoy.

JANET: But narrow, looking back, like the railway lines
Twisting behind you. The journey could end
At any moment—it could be now,
All unexpected, just as it was for him.

ROBERT: We need to forget that, and begin with tomorrow—
You said it yourself—as though nothing had happened.

JANET: We have done our best to forgive
And to understand—his ghost should be satisfied.
Would you be afraid, if we saw him here, now,
Standing between us—or lying covered with blood
As when he died? I half dread it:
His violent piteous death is still a shadow.

ROBERT: My dear old girl, you must come into the daylight,
You must think that the sun is at the top of heaven
And casts no shadows.

JANET: I feel as though he had been thrown into the sea
With no provision—his ship of death—
He had no time to provision it, Robert!

ROBERT: What can I do to comfort you, my dear?
What can I say?

JANET: Nothing. Unless . . .
You mustn't laugh at me. . . . When we were small
I sometimes used to make you join in a charm—
A kind of incantation. Do you remember that?

ROBERT: Yes, I remember. I never much liked it:
You believed it so thoroughly, I used to be afraid
We should—call up something. You don't mean to try?

JANET: O no, no, not that. For don't you remember,
I did it quite often when we were afraid,
To make us safe. Couldn't you help me
To speed him on his voyage now—provision his ship?

ROBERT: Very well, I'll try.

JANET: We must join our hands.

ROBERT: Now. You begin.

JANET: For the dead, we pray
That the wrongs he suffered
Forgiven, may vanish:

ROBERT: Not cherished in memory
Clinging like limpets
Drag at his keel.

JANET: That the wrongs he committed
Forgiven, may vanish:

ROBERT: Not follow like ghosts
To bewilder his passage.

JANET: May he, accepting
The outrage of death
Be free of its meaning.
May the wine of our pardon

ROBERT: The bread of our pardon

JANET: Provision the voyage.

ROBERT: At every stage

JANET: May the Holy Spirit
Enliven the sails.

ROBERT: After the fog of pain

JANET: The icy shock
As soul splits from sense

ROBERT: May the ship drive forward.

JANET: May he go boldly

ROBERT: To Arctic regions
Of different being.

JANET: May Christ be his shield
Against the Eternal Light!

CURTAIN

How Bitter the Bread

Tu proverai sì come sa di sale
lo pane altrui, e com'è duro calle
lo scendere e il salir per l'altrui scale.
Dante: Paradiso *XVII, 58.*

To

E. L. WAGER

and her Little Gaddesden players

AUTHOR'S NOTE

This brief play was written at the request of Oliver Wilkinson, for production with the minimum of props—even if necessary in halls with no stage. It lasts about twenty minutes. Acknowledgements are due to the Quarterly Review of the Community of the Resurrection, Mirfield, where the play was first printed.

CHARACTERS

ALEXIS

JOHN

BARBARA

CATHERINE

ANN

BLIND MAN

PROLOGUE

(optional for production)

You shall find how bitter is the taste of bread in a strange house, and how hard a journey it is to go up and down the stairway belonging to another.

Where will it end, the line of refugees,
Men and women, trudging the roadways,
Carrying bundles, carrying babies,
Dying by the roadside? Where will it end? . . .
The line goes as far as memory can reach
Or thought can pierce the future.
For years ago the glass was turned,
Glass ball with its image of a peaceful scene
Turned upside down, and the snowflake fugitives
Whirling, darkening the face of Europe,
Blot out the lights and the village green.

On one side of the acting space, the three women knitting squares, and JOHN *sorting bundles of clothes and putting them into sacks. On the other,* ALEXIS *sitting on a knapsack. If there is no curtain,* ALEXIS *should enter, and fling down the pack (with modification as below in his first lines), and the others should enter on* ANN'S *first line, and settle to work as they talk.*

ALEXIS: Down on his luck. Here he is
Sitting down on his luck—all that's left of it:*
[*Kneels and begins to rummage in his pack*]
One pair socks, one pair pants,
And the necessary badge of respectability—
A cake of soap. All was charity,
And none of it began at home.
[*He eats a piece of bread.*]
Lonely bread—it's in need of a helpmate.
Now, if I imagined the soap to be cheese,
How far would my imagination take me?
Bread of exile, bread of charity—
How bitterly it tastes!
[*He continues to eat, while the focus shifts to the others.*]

ANN: O yes, charity begins at home,
But the trouble with me is—I've a tender conscience:
Knitting these shawls is not enough,
I felt I must at least *offer* hospitality.

BARBARA: Can a starving wanderer eat your conscience,
Or sit beside it and keep himself warm?
I somehow doubt it.

ANN: And yet, Barbara,
Did *you* do more?

BARBARA: O, not so much,
Ann my dear, I don't uphold
My own example—I only say
One ought to know one's limitations.

* *or* There it goes:
Down goes his luck, all that's left of it.

CATHERINE: The trouble with both of you is—you're amateurs.
John and I have given our lives
To this kind of work, and we know what it means.
You can't hold anything back from this,
Can you, John?
[JOHN *grunts from his corner.*]
I know at once
When I go to a house that has offered hospitality
Whether it's the right sort of place or not.
No good clinging to the best armchair,
The wing of the chicken, the nook by the fire—

BARBARA: And privacy—that's what I can't dispense with.

CATHERINE: You've got to share everything.

BARBARA: What about your husband?

CATHERINE: Don't be silly, Barbara.

ANN: Seriously though
What *about* him? Whilst you are clothing the naked,
John's socks are full of holes—he needs a clean collar.

CATHERINE: Do I neglect you, John?

JOHN: It is part of the agreement:
We chose this work; we knew what it meant—
Facilis descensus, to an unmade bed;
Facile prandium, out of a tin.
That's understood. But how do *they* feel it?
However hard we try, we can't really know:
We know it in theory, we know it in poetry—
'Here we have no abiding City . . .'
[*The light is focused on* ALEXIS.]

ALEXIS [*simultaneously with* JOHN]:
'Here we have no abiding City'.
Waters flow, wheels go,
Pilgrims know the goal they're seeking,
Travellers, birds and bees are homing,
But refugees move round and round,
Travel ever without arriving.

Home! Keep off that word. Don't think of it.
Move on there, if you please. Keep moving:
That train is full of others who need
This yard of earth you're occupying.
[*He gets up and begins to walk in a circle.*]
All I *want* is to keep moving;
If I were still I might remember—
I might remember what is lost.
Let me not dream, or think, or feel,
But freeze my heart and keep moving.
First the camp, then the train,
Then the station, then the camp.*
Moving on becomes a habit,
Soon you lose the knack of stopping,
Soon there's nothing left but moving,
Unless you fall down dead . . .
[*He has moved and spoken in a crescendo, till he crosses the stage and is caught in the outstretched arms of* JOHN.]

ALL THE OTHERS: Stop!

CATHERINE: Come in. You are safe here;
Out of danger. Nothing but welcome;
Peace and welcome. All are friends here.

ALEXIS: You are very kind. Please forgive me:
I can't get my bearings.

JOHN: Take it easy,
There is no hurry.

ALEXIS: Either the world
Has come unstuck, or . . . *Am* I going round
Like a top?

BARBARA: No, but sit down here.
I guess how you feel: like waking in the dark
At the wrong end of the bed—finding no anchorage,
As though one fell like a falling star,
Whirling through black space.

* (Repeat ad lib if needed.)

ALEXIS: The flakes begin to settle.
They turned us upside down, you see,
Like a snowstorm in a bottle—we all went flying—
Saw nothing but fugitives. *You* seem to be fixed,
And the air is clearing.

CATHERINE: Yes, your troubles are nearly over.

ALEXIS: Are they really?

BARBARA: Don't tell him that:
'How bitter is the bread in another's house,
How hard the stairway . . .' He ought to be prepared.
Mr . . .?

ALEXIS: My name is Alexis.

BARBARA: Alexis:
This is Catherine, her husband, John;
This is Ann; and my name is Barbara.
We all want to help. If you go to Ann,
She will do her very best, but you *may* discover
You are driving her crazy. If you go to Catherine . . .

JOHN: In our house there is always a breeze,
Always movement, everyone too busy
To sit by the fire, or think about food—
We stoke up in passing. But you are accustomed
To railway stations—you will feel at home.

ALEXIS: What about yourself, Miss Barbara?
Do you offer me a home?

BARBARA: I am too selfish,
Too much set in my ways to share a home.
I offer you money—all that I can.

ALEXIS: So I am free to choose. You are very kind . . .

BARBARA: Don't put it too high. You offer us the chance
Of doing a good deed that won't hurt us too much.
We all fear conversion. And you're a kind of insurance—
One day we too might need help . . .

JOHN: I prefer
Not to analyse my motives—I don't like what I find there.

ALEXIS: And I prefer you not to: you might think of me!
I don't want to be your insurance
Or your painless good deed: I am myself—Alexis.
I am alive, at least—and that is quite something
In the place where I came from.

CATHERINE: Then choose, Alexis:
Which of us shall have you?
[*They draw apart from one another.*]

ALEXIS: I don't know what to answer.

BARBARA: Toss for it, then.

ANN: Here is a choice of three, but a coin has only two.
[*Enter* BLIND MAN, *unseen at first by them.*]

ALEXIS: Blindfold me, then, and turn me well round,
And whichever one I touch shall be—the lucky one.
I shall catch him, but he will have caught me.
What a prize! How fine to confer such benefits!

CATHERINE [*putting a scarf round his head*]:
Now, you mustn't be bitter. *You* must be generous too.
Is everything dark? You can't see a thing?

ALEXIS: No, nothing at all.

CATHERINE: I turn you round and—now, make your catch.
[*The* BLIND MAN *walks across* ALEXIS'S *path:* ALEXIS *seizes him and he cries out.*]

BLIND MAN: Are you blind? Didn't you see me?
Surely you can see that I've got no stick?

ALEXIS: Who is it that I've caught? [*tearing off the scarf*]

BLIND MAN: People as a rule
Keep out of my way. It wouldn't have happened,
But some devil of a boy ran off with my stick.
I am lost without it—lost in the dark
Like a star that's unfixed.

ALEXIS: Strange you should say that:
I know what that means. Shall I lead you home?

BLIND MAN: But have you your sight?

ALEXIS: Why, I possess five senses
Besides my life! I'm rich!

BLIND MAN: Then I gladly accept
The help of a rich man.

CATHERINE [*to* ALEXIS]: How can you help him?
It's just a ridiculous idea. How
Can you take him home when you don't know the way?
[*to* BLIND MAN] I'm afraid he can't help you. He was only joking.

BLIND MAN: Is he strange to the town? That doesn't matter.
I know the way all right: I just need someone
To take me along it.

ALEXIS: And when you reach home,
What could I do? Could I still be useful?

BLIND MAN: You could stay for a while and see how you liked it.

ALEXIS: But could I help you?

BLIND MAN: A man with five senses?
There's plenty you could do, of course. But you wouldn't stop long:
You'd soon get tired of me. I tell you, for one thing,
I talk in my sleep. And I repeat my stories—
Or so they say.

ALEXIS: I've only one story—
A sad one. I'd like to learn some others.

BLIND MAN: Well, come, then.
We must be getting home.

ALEXIS [*to the rest*]: Thank you, all of you. I shan't forget your kindness.
But to be needed—that is best of all.

I might travel a thousand miles and not find it;
I might wait through a dozen years for such a chance.
I must take it. Good-bye. And once more, thank you:
Thank you with all my heart.

BLIND MAN: Are you ready now?
I'll show you how we do it:
Let me put my hand on your arm—so.
Now just walk normally: I shall keep up.

BARBARA: Good-bye, Alexis.

CATHERINE: Good-bye, Alexis. I hope you'll manage.

JOHN: Good-bye, Alexis.
[ANN *follows the* BLIND MAN *and* ALEXIS *to the exit.*]

ANN [*looking after them*]: They're going all right—but now they have to cross.
I hope he remembers the rule of the road.

JOHN [*joining her*]: He doesn't! He's looking in the wrong direction!

ANN: There's a car! Thank goodness, they stopped in time.

BARBARA: The blind man will get him home safely, no doubt.

CATHERINE: And what if he doesn't?

BARBARA: I'd prefer to take the risk
If I were Alexis, I know that.

ANN: O, good,
Now they are well across. Good-bye, Alexis. [*Waving.*]

ALL: Good-bye, Alexis. God be with you, Alexis.

CATHERINE: I hope we were wise to let them go.

BARBARA [*rolling up her knitting*]: A yellow square finished—that was Alexis.
I've knitted him into it, and now he's cast off.

ANN: Don't put it like that! He was a nice boy.
I half wish I had taken him . . .

CATHERINE: Do you think we have failed him, John?

JOHN: He took the best offer.
I say this prayer for him, before the next one comes,
And for that next one too, and for all the others:
Though he has lost everything, may he find a home—
A place to start from.

BARBARA: May the stranger's bread
Taste sweet to him, and the way be easy.

ANN: May he go in peace.

CATHERINE: And may God go with him.

THE END